SOCIAL NETWORK-POWERED EMPLOYMENT OPPORTUNITIES

MONIQUE VESCIA

ROSEN
PUBLISHING®

New York

Published in 2014 by The Rosen Publishing Group, Inc.
29 East 21st Street, New York, NY 10010

First Edition

Library of Congress Cataloging-in-Publication Data

Vescia, Monique.
Social network–powered employment opportunities/
Monique Vescia.—First edition.
    pages cm.—(A teen's guide to the power of social networking)
Includes bibliographical references and index.
ISBN 978-1-4777-1683-0 (library binding)—
ISBN 978-1-4777-1913-8 (pbk.)—
ISBN 978-1-4777-1914-5 (6-pack)
1. Job hunting—Computer network resources. 2. Teenagers—Employment. 3. Online social networks. 4. Social media.
I. Title.
HF5382.7.V48 2014
650.140285'4678—dc23
                                                    2013011264

Manufactured in Malaysia

CPSIA Compliance Information: Batch #W14YA: For further information, contact Rosen Publishing, New York, New York, at 1-800-237-9932.

CONTENTS

INTRODUCTION

Every job seeker has heard, at one point or another, the following words: "It's all about who you know." It's a cliché because it's true. Social networks are as old as human history, and young people have always relied on the guidance and referrals of family and friends—and friends of friends—to help launch their careers. So while many people have said that a person's success in the job market depends on the strength of his or her social connections, you may not realize that job hunters today have a huge advantage. In the early years of the twenty-first century, the evolution of the Internet means that people's interconnectivity can extend far beyond their immediate family, friends, and geographical community.

The majority of teenagers today spend about five hours a day online, staying in constant touch with friends via texts and Twitter messages, or tweets. They send goofy images to each other's smartphones and surf through cyberspace like they were born there—which they practically were.

Most teens already belong to virtual communities that include many hundreds or even millions of people, from all over the country…or even the planet. They can also use all of those connections, as well as the skills they've developed navigating online social networks, to help them find a job. Furthermore, the social media industry itself is busy generating a wealth of new opportunities for young people just entering the job market.

Lani Lazzari started with an e-mail list and a good idea and used her social connections to build a business. She suffers from eczema, a medical condition that causes skin

By allowing users to connect with a much wider community, social networks help today's job hunters lay the virtual foundations for a successful employment search.

irritation, and since commercial products tended to irritate her skin further, she decided to create her own version of a salt scrub using ingredients that she purchased from a local Whole Foods store. Her product worked beautifully and was a big hit with family members who received jars of her homemade scrub as Christmas gifts.

The scrub might have remained just another personal project, but eleven-year-old Lani used her networking skills to launch a thriving business. Starting with an e-mail list of family and friends, she established a base of loyal customers. She expanded her product line and enlisted family members to help make the scrubs in her parents' Pittsburgh, Pennsylvania, basement. Then Lani started a Web site to publicize and sell Simple Sugars, her all-natural face and body scrubs for sensitive skin. She networked offline, too, to market her skincare products. While in high school, Lani embarked on a six-week cross-country trip to promote her brand, which is now sold at—you guessed it—Whole Foods.

Not everyone has entrepreneurial aspirations, but each individual has a personal "brand" that she or he can publicize and promote. Social networks such as Facebook, LinkedIn, and Twitter are powerful personal marketing platforms that let job seekers pitch themselves to prospective employers. A professional and active online presence can attract employers and recruiters to potential job candidates as well.

Whether they are planning on a career on- or offline, social networking can help job seekers find the jobs they want, research the companies that interest them, and connect with the people who work there.

CHAPTER 1

SOCIAL MEDIA AND THE JOB MARKET

Not so long ago, most job hunters spent hours poring over employment listings in local newspapers. They snail-mailed résumés and cover letters to dozens of employers. If they were lucky enough to land a job, they may have spent years—or a lifetime—with the same company.

In our brave new digital world, job seekers more often apply for jobs online. They use a variety of powerful search engines that scan the Internet—in mere seconds—for job listings filtered by industry, title, salary range, and geographical location. Job candidates may submit their résumés on video and be interviewed via the teleconferencing software Skype rather than in person. They typically spend less than a year in one position before hopping to another job. Most career coaches say that online networking is, by far, the most effective way of looking for employment.

For anyone born around the turn of the millennium, social networks are a part of daily life, a common method of social interaction. Most Facebook users wouldn't think of going a day without logging onto their pages to check their friends' status updates on the News Feed.

The most popular social networking platform is Facebook, which has more than a billion members. That means one in seven people on the planet today is a Facebook user. Facebook has changed the way that people relate to one another and has added a new word—"unfriend"—to the dictionary. It has been a key factor in recent political uprisings and humanitarian relief efforts all over the world.

Perhaps because of Facebook's unique success, the playing field for social media has widened. Users have been quick to adopt new social media and microblogging platforms such as

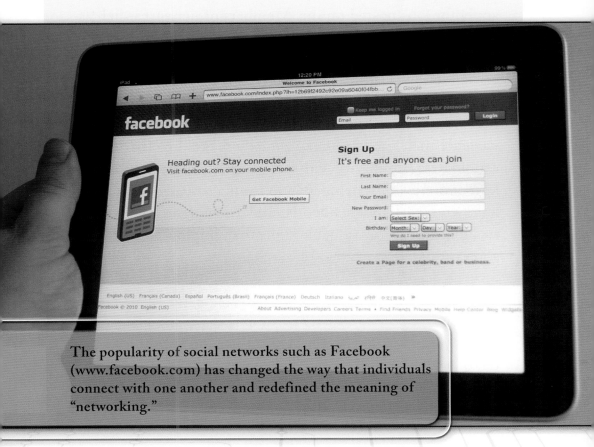

The popularity of social networks such as Facebook (www.facebook.com) has changed the way that individuals connect with one another and redefined the meaning of "networking."

Twitter, on which tweets allow rapid-fire, real-time communication between millions of users. Image-heavy networks such as Tumblr and Pinterest are among the more recent guests at the party. New applications enable users to easily integrate their networks so that they can feed content from their Facebook accounts to Twitter or Tumblr and back.

The influence of social networks on how people communicate has handed job hunters an incredibly powerful tool. Social networks can help speed up job searching by enabling job seekers to research different career choices and companies. They can quickly and easily search for and apply for jobs posted online. Members of networks such as LinkedIn receive job notices forwarded directly to their e-mail inboxes. Individuals can share job listings with friends via Facebook or Twitter. Some may dismiss social networking as a huge time-waster, and it most certainly can be. But here's the surprising thing: the skills teens develop as they navigate social networks can actually make them better job candidates. Familiarity with computer technologies and fast keyboarding skills; being able to think critically, solve problems, and work independently; and knowing how to use social media are all valuable skills that employers look for in a job candidate.

Social Recruiting

Employers and recruiters have fully awakened to the potential of social networks as a recruiting tool. "Social recruiting" is a common buzz phrase in human resources (HR)

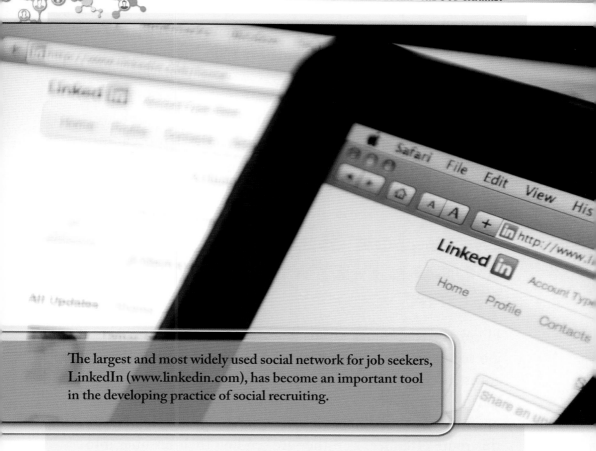

The largest and most widely used social network for job seekers, LinkedIn (www.linkedin.com), has become an important tool in the developing practice of social recruiting.

circles. Companies that use social media to recruit report lower employee turnover than those that do not, according to a recent "Social Media Effectiveness Report" from the recruitment service the A-List. This suggests that employees who are hired through social media are happier in their jobs than those hired by traditional methods. Employers and recruiters can search for, identify, and evaluate someone as a potential job candidate based on her or his online presence.

They can tap current employees for references to friends and family members who are looking for a job. They can even reach out to individuals who aren't actively searching for work, known as passive candidates. Employers send tweets advertising their current job offerings. They communicate about the culture and work environment of their organization in hopes of attracting qualified individuals. So clearly, anyone still looking for a job the old-fashioned way is at a disadvantage.

How Job Seekers Use Social Networks to Find Work

Here's the traditional approach to searching for a job: the job seeker finds an advertised position, submits a résumé and cover letter, and waits for a response. Recruiters call this the "push" method, and it's not particularly effective. In an economy where competition for jobs is fierce, applicants who go this route often feel as if they are sending their résumés into a giant black hole. Employers rarely contact them to confirm that they've received an application or to inform them that the position has been given to someone else.

In contrast, the "pull" method attempts to attract employers and recruiters to the job seeker. Social media has sped up that process. Recently, Internmatch.com, a company that helps students find internships, ran a "Kill the Cover Letter" campaign. It wanted to encourage job seekers to dump traditional job-hunting methods in favor of using social media. Participants in the campaign who used Facebook, Twitter, and WordPress were five times more likely to receive a job offer than those who sent in cover letters and résumés.

Job hunters who want to use social media to their advantage, regardless of which networks they belong to, must do the following:

- Become a member (most networks are free to join)
- Create a personal profile
- Send invitations to and accept invitations from other members

Thanks to mobile smartphone apps, Twitter users can actively search for job postings in the "Twitterverse." They can also attract the attention of potential employers by sending tweets.

- Search for contacts
- Join groups

Each of the major social networks profiled here can aid in the job search by helping job seekers make useful social contacts and build relationships on- and offline. These tools will help them polish their digital presence and promote their own brand. Finally, they are an excellent resource for information about specific employers and the positions they're looking to fill. If you already belong to one or more of these networks, be sure to find out the latest resources and applications offered for job seekers. The following information should provide you with a starting point.

FACEBOOK

Although a personal Facebook page might seem like a private space, more people are starting to use it as a job-hunting platform. Facebook has its Social Jobs app, which lets users search more than a million job openings from a hub on the site. Facebook members can easily connect with a huge network of members and find groups of people with whom they share common interests, a great way to expand one's professional networks.

The Graph Search function allows users to conduct highly specific searches, such as "People who work at [company] who like snowboarding." Names with whom a member has the most connections will appear at the top of the search results, providing that person with potentially useful information for a job search, and maybe even a great way to break the ice with a hiring manager.

How does Graph Search work?

Mark Zuckerberg, founder and CEO of Facebook, proudly takes the stage to introduce the social network's new Graph Search function.

A Facebook profile can incorporate multimedia content, a real advantage for artistic people who want to show off their work. For a reasonable fee, members can even post ads announcing their availability to targeted areas of the Facebook community. Employers who search for job candidates on Facebook will expect their pages to be more creative and less formal than the profiles on LinkedIn or another professional networking site.

If you currently have a personal account that you'd also like to use for your job search, you can revamp your profile to ensure that the content posted on your page is appropriate and will appeal to potential employers and then adjust your privacy settings. Or you can choose to maintain separate accounts—one for professional networking and one for personal networking, using a nickname or another version of your name.

Customize your privacy settings so that only friends and family can view your personal profile. When you create your professional profile, leave fields blank that ask for information that isn't relevant to a job search and which shouldn't be publicly available: your birth year, address, phone number, and religious and political views. Once you've set up your site, monitor it regularly to be sure that no one has posted anything on your wall that might detract from your professional image.

Some Facebook users have been alarmed when potential employers have asked them to divulge passwords to their private accounts as a condition of being considered for a job. Employers claim they have a right to know exactly whom they are hiring, but courts have called such requests an invasion of privacy. As of the time of this writing, six U.S. states had passed legislation that prohibits companies from demanding access to private social networking accounts.

LINKEDIN

LinkedIn actually predates Facebook by about three years and has developed an excellent reputation as the world's largest professional networking site. Human resources experts advise that if a job seeker plans to use just one platform for professional networking, LinkedIn should be it. This diverse network includes everyone from entry-level workers and high-level executives to the unemployed and self-employed in more than two hundred countries. Unlike on Facebook and Twitter, one must be at least eighteen to become a member of LinkedIn.

LinkedIn uses a powerful search engine that lets members find former classmates and work colleagues, whom they can invite to join their networks. They receive e-mails from other members inviting them to join their networks. A member may choose to be selective about which invitations he or she accepts, or opt to be a LinkedIn Open Networker, called a LION. LinkedIn LIONs accept all invitations from network members, whether they know them personally or not. LinkedIn users can find groups made up of others who share their interests or background. They can also broadcast questions to their network, which means that each member potentially has access to a whole range of expertise.

In addition to searching for jobs on the site, users can look for contacts that might be able to give them inside information about a specific job or a leg up in the hiring process. LinkedIn also lets members research companies and access useful information, such as the names of people in their networks who work there or those who have recently left the company. Over time, this powerful networking platform will undoubtedly add new features and technologies to benefit its growing community of users.

TWO GREAT WAYS TO GET NOTICED

In a competitive job market, job seekers have had to get highly creative in order to attract an employer's eye. Attention-getting techniques are not new, but social media offers an innovative set of tools that clever job hunters can use to their advantage. For instance, one job hunter took out a Google ad featuring the name of a New York ad agency executive. When the executive searched for his name on Google, the ad—with the hunter's job request—popped up at the top of the page. This ingenuity won him an interview, and he was eventually hired by the agency.

One out-of-work college grad got fed up with sending out job applications and never hearing back from employers. Then he had a brainstorm: he decided to turn the whole process on its head and create a "reverse job application." He listed his criteria for a potential employer and requested that recruiters submit an employer application form. Interested hiring managers had to answer a series of questions, including, "What job are you offering me?" The college grad posted his reverse application on the social news site Reddit. When he woke up the next morning, his in-box was stuffed with responses.

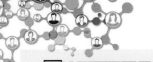

TWITTER

Twitter is a different breed of network from the other sites. While both Facebook and LinkedIn are closed systems, where members can only communicate directly with people in their network, Twitter is open to everyone. Tweets (short posts limited to 140 characters or fewer) can be sent from a computer or a cell phone in real time, and users can communicate and build relationships with anyone in the Twitterverse. Launched in 2006, Twitter caught on quickly with celebrities, politicians, and others who benefit from keeping themselves in the public eye. Journalists use Twitter to access and share breaking news as it happens. Even highly traditional organizations now acknowledge the importance of Twitter. The Catholic Church officially announced the election of Pope Francis on Twitter, and the Library of Congress now archives tweets.

Even people who already use Twitter (also known as tweeps) might be surprised to learn that the network can be used as a job-searching platform. Actually, career consultants consider Twitter one of the best and most underutilized tools that a job seeker can use. When setting up a Twitter profile, you should use the same photo that you use for other networking accounts in order to keep your online brand consistent. Then customize your profile background to reflect the kind of image you want to convey. Your character bio is limited to 160 characters, so every word has to count. You want to craft a sales pitch that will make you stand out in the Twitterverse.

Begin by "following" people who interest you: industry leaders, experts in a particular field, recruiters, and others you can find by clicking the Find People tab in Twitter. Read their tweets to learn what's capturing their interest and what they're discussing with others on Twitter. Comment on their posts, and let them know what you think about what they're tweeting. Create links and retweet worthwhile updates, one of the highest compliments you can pay another tweep. Follow the Twitter accounts for companies you'd like to work for as well. Creating lists (a feature of the site) of the people and organizations you follow will help you organize your employment search.

It's not enough to just be a follower, though—you also want to spark a following of your own. That means regularly contributing to the conversation and replying to messages quickly. But whether you're tweeting a funny quote, sharing a cool picture, or joining a discussion, remember to limit your "I" and "me" statements: "you" messages, such as "Do you think traditional résumés are obsolete?" get retweeted more often than "I"s. And don't forget that Twitter is a very public forum—you should never tweet any personal information (birth date, phone number, address) or messages that reflect poorly on you or a former employer.

Hashtags, words or phrases preceded by the pound sign (#), help organize the chaos of information on Twitter. Searching for hashtags such as #jobpostings, #employment, and #hiring will help a job hunter find positions posted on the network. Employers and recruiters also do keyword searches on Twitter to hunt for job candidates, so use hashtags with industry-specific terms in your tweets. Finally, check out some of the growing number of Twitter apps that can help you refine your use of this job-hunting resource.

OTHER SOCIAL NETWORKS FOR JOB HUNTERS

Facebook, LinkedIn, and Twitter may be the best-known social networks utilized by job seekers, but they aren't the only sites worth investigating. Launched in June 2011, Google+ (pronounced "Google Plus") is Google's social networking platform. The site has nowhere near Facebook's one billion users, but users like its Circles feature and the fact that there are no friend requests. You can easily add or remove anyone from a given circle at any time simply by dragging and dropping them where you want them. The network also has a useful feature that allows members to see how their profile appears to different people.

Tumblr is another user-friendly social networking platform for job hunters, especially those seeking work in creative professions. This blogging platform makes it easy to add all kinds of content, from images and videos to audio posts. As on Twitter, users can follow other members and use hashtags to help employers find their content.

A virtual bulletin board where users "pin" various items that interest them, Pinterest attracts many influential designers, marketers, and advertisers. This image-heavy site is a great platform for displaying a visual portfolio or promoting a personal blog.

Google, the search engine that is now a household word, launched its own social media platform. Google+ (plus .google.com) surpassed Twitter to become the world's second largest social network.

Other professional networking sites worth a visit include Brazen Careerist and Xing, an international version of LinkedIn.

RESEARCHING PROSPECTIVE EMPLOYERS ONLINE

Employers can use the Internet to investigate you, but you can do the same to them—and you should. Many businesses and companies today maintain a Facebook page or a tumblelog as part of their public relations (PR) strategy. Job seekers should check out these sites to see what they can learn. Bear in mind, though, that these pages present an image that an organization wants people to see. To get the whole picture, warts and all, dig a little deeper. Useful sites that provide information about companies include Job-Hunt.org, Vault.com, and Glassdoor.com, where job hunters can access data about different companies, including salary information, posted anonymously by employees.

The field of social media is incredibly dynamic. New technologies and tools will continue to burst on the scene, so stay current and knowledgeable about the latest recruitment trends and new ways to power a job search.

CHAPTER 2

ONLINE BRANDING FOR JOB CANDIDATES

Anyone who regularly uses the Internet leaves a digital footprint for others to follow. When someone signs an online petition, e-mails a letter to the editor of a magazine, or comments on a funny picture posted by a friend, that person's name and sometimes his or her image can wind up on the Internet, available to anyone to find with a few mouse clicks. Horror stories abound about employees who have lost their jobs when a derogatory tweet or posting on Facebook went viral. An overwhelming majority of employers conduct online searches of potential employees, and many continue to search after an employee has been hired. Getting caught posting pictures of yourself gleefully rock climbing on the day you called in sick with the stomach flu is the type of misstep that has earned employees a pink slip. In fact, this happens so often that there's now a term for it: "Facebook fired."

However, there are other things that job hunters might not want to reveal on the Internet because they might influence how prospective employers see them. For instance, a job seeker with a disability may prefer to disclose information

Every Internet user creates a unique digital footprint when navigating the Web. Job seekers can take steps to ensure their online persona creates a favorable impression.

about a condition on his or her own time, rather than having an employer learn about it from an online search. A transgender employee may prefer to keep his or her transgender status private.

Sometimes what isn't there can reflect poorly on an individual, as well. If an Internet search for your name turns up only outdated information (say, a tagged photo of you dressed as a mushroom in your preschool pageant), it suggests that you're not very connected or involved in your community and, frankly, not very remarkable. So you owe it to yourself to investigate your own online presence to see if you would want to hire the person that you find there.

CONDUCT AN ONLINE AUDIT OF YOURSELF

To determine what potential employers might discover when they search for you online, start by searching for yourself. First, log out of your accounts or choose a browser that you're not already logged into; otherwise, the results will be customized for your personal profile. Type your first and last name into the search box and see what pops up at the top of the search results. Go a few pages deep, but don't waste your time checking every single result. You should also search your public self on Facebook, LinkedIn, Twitter, and Google+.

If your name is a common one, an online search might pull up a lot of content related to other people who share that name. You can begin to create a unique digital identity for yourself by adding a middle initial or middle name to all of your online transactions. Establishing a strong digital presence is one way to make sure that the "Michael Johnson" at the top of the search results is you.

An increasing number of companies specializing in "reputation management" will investigate and clean up an online persona…for a price. It's a lot less expensive to avoid posting questionable stuff in the first place. A good rule of thumb is to never post any words or images online that you wouldn't be comfortable showing to anyone, including your little brother or your great-aunt. If you just can't help yourself from posting embarrassing photos and sending rude tweets, you might want to consider getting some "Internet shame insurance," a simple extension for Google Chrome that will add privacy reminders to your Facebook, Twitter, and Gmail accounts. When you're about to post a status update or hit Reply All, a message pops up to remind you to stop and consider the possible (and public) ramifications of your actions.

Your online presence should be a favorable reflection of your personality. When you curate it—that is, highlight the material that shows you in your best light—bear in mind that the goal is not to remove all traces of individuality and interest from your profile. You don't want to scrub your image so clean that you come across as robotically bland or devoid of social skills, either. What you should aim for is something that career guru Joshua Waldman calls "the public private." Waldman points out that newscasters and others who cultivate a public persona make a point of sharing

Michael Fertik, CEO of Reputation.com, is in the growing field of reputation management. Fertik's thriving company helps individuals investigate and polish their online personas.

details about their lives, information that encourages viewers to feel as if they know them, but which are not so private as to be potentially embarrassing. Your online presence can include playful images and personal posts, but these should be fit for public consumption.

ENHANCING YOUR ONLINE PRESENCE

Once you've joined one or more social networks and established your profile on these sites, your next step should be to enhance your personal brand. One approach, mentioned earlier, involves getting rid of your "digital dirt," or the content that reflects poorly on you or doesn't add luster to the brand you want to create. Another approach is to make sure that plenty of positive content about you or generated by you is the first thing a potential employer finds when he or she Googles your name.

The Internet provides you with a world of ways to add content by asking good questions, sharing your knowledge and enthusiasm, helping others connect with one another, and otherwise contributing value to the online community. The types of digital information you do want a prospective employee to discover online can include blogs that you host, your comments on other people's blogs, your tweets, and content you've shared by retweeting and reblogging.

BLOGS

Blogging is a great way to enhance your digital presence. Hosted blogging platforms such as Blogger, WordPress, and

Tumblr are user-friendly and let you easily upload all types of content, including text, photos, quotes, chats, audio, and video. The subject or focus of your blog should be something that you're truly passionate about. Someone aspiring to a career in marine biology might start a blog about nudibranchs and post images of these colorful sea slugs along with links to online discussions or taped scientific lectures about these fascinating creatures. Having her blog pop up first in the search results when a hiring manager Googles her name would give the blogger an advantage when applying for a job at the local aquarium.

There are a couple of things to keep in mind if you're considering starting your own blog: it's a commitment, since you'll want to post regularly. Remember, too, that blogs invite discussion, and you should be willing to productively engage with people who comment on yours. Unlike in a discussion group, the blog owner is the main author who establishes the blog's subject matter and sets the tone. And don't forget to include links on your blog to your various social network profiles.

Blogging platforms, such as Tumblr (www.tumblr.com), can be used to create a positive presence on the Web. Members can upload various types of content to make their blogs stand out.

COMMENTING ON OTHERS' BLOGS

Blogs are terrific forums for people who enjoy writing, but if the written word isn't your strong suit, you're probably better off commenting on other existing blogs. Take the time to identify those most relevant to your goals or interests. Before you submit any comments, get a sense for the tone of the comments that other blog readers have submitted. Your comment will become a permanent part of a blog's archives, so be sure it's relevant, respectful, and free from grammatical and spelling errors. Keep in mind that the goal is not to trumpet your own accomplishments but to make a useful contribution to the blogosphere. You should also include links to your social network profiles so that interested readers can find out more about you.

TWEETS

Twitter is another great forum for people who don't enjoy blogging or writing longer posts. While its 140-character limit (and its hyper-public nature) does force users to choose their words with care, these little sound bites can have a big impact and quickly go viral. Good things to tweet about include the type of job you're interested in, industry events and trends, new skills you've learned, and an interesting book or article you've read. Find out what the trending keywords are in your career field and use them with a hashtag in your tweets. Your Twitter account can be linked with your other networks. You can also integrate Twitter with your smartphone so that

FACEBOOK FIRED

Even in this day and age, it's amazing how often employees forget that Facebook and other social media networks are public forums and that everyone—including the people they work for—can see what goes on there. In 2007, a Canadian grocery chain fired seven of its employees when it learned that they had created a derogatory Facebook page. On that page, some employees posted insults about customers and bad-mouthed the company.

Two employees at a Massachusetts nonprofit organization lost their jobs when a photo they posted on Facebook went viral and caused a scandal. The image, taken at Arlington National Cemetery, showed one of the employees pretending to yell and making an obscene gesture next to a sign requesting silence and respect.

Those are both pretty stupid mistakes, but some people should definitely know better. A social media strategist at the car company Chrysler got fired when he posted an offensive tweet about bad drivers in Detroit, Michigan. Even worse, he accidentally sent the tweet from the car manufacturer's corporate account!

you won't miss a DM (direct message). Job seekers who demonstrate an active Twitter presence have a distinct advantage over those who don't, so be sure to tweet regularly.

SHARING USEFUL DIGITAL CONTENT

A key feature of social media networks is the ability to share content with other members, which can help build goodwill and relationships within the online community. Retweeting

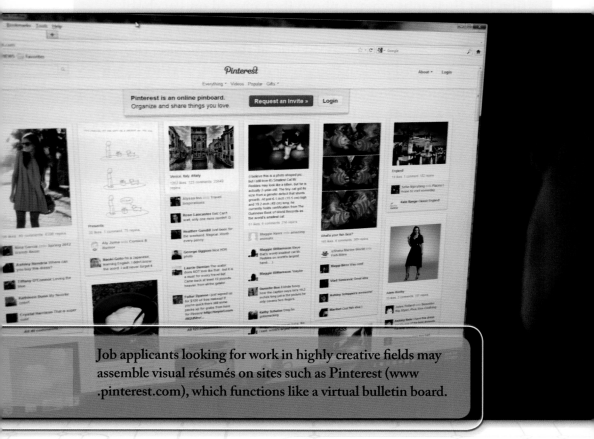

Job applicants looking for work in highly creative fields may assemble visual résumés on sites such as Pinterest (www .pinterest.com), which functions like a virtual bulletin board.

someone's post on Twitter is a nice thing to do and may spark a relationship with a fellow tweep. That person will often return the compliment by retweeting one of your posts, which increases your digital visibility. The "like" and "reblog" buttons on Tumblr and the "repin" function on Pinterest allow you to publically approve and share others' posts on your own site.

Finally, a word on social media etiquette. In cyberspace, certain rules of conduct do apply, and you'd be wise to heed them if you want to be seen as a responsible citizen of the Web. If someone follows you on Twitter, for instance, it's polite to follow that person back. When you share content, join a conversation, or comment on someone's post, your goal should always be to bring something worthwhile to the "cyber-table." When employers search for you online, they'll be impressed by what they find there.

CHAPTER 3

CYBERPATHS TO WEB-BASED WORK

Long famous for its coffee, Starbucks has also become known for its stellar social media strategy. The company's master plan includes a Starbucks YouTube Channel, a Facebook page with millions of fans, a Twitter account, a blog, and the company's own social network called My Starbucks Idea, where customers can share suggestions and vote on others' ideas.

Like Starbucks, a growing number of organizations and companies are budgeting generously for social media, and positions in the field have grown. According to the job board site Indeed.com, job postings over the past year that included the phrase "social media" increased by a whopping 88 percent.

The digital revolution has created new career paths. It has also helped render many traditional jobs nearly obsolete. While many blame the Internet for the sharp decline in print journalism and the diminishing number of positions for newspaper reporters and magazine editors, there has been a surge in jobs for bloggers, e-newsletter editors, and Web content generators. Another sign of the changing times are gimmicky job titles such as "social media wizard," "ghost tweeter," and "brand ambassador."

If you're obsessed with online networking and think you would enjoy working in the swiftly evolving field of social media, plenty of employers would love to hear from you. Because the industry is still relatively young, a job seeker's passion counts more than his or her experience. However, anyone aspiring to these jobs should have an active presence on Facebook, Twitter, and other social networks. Good candidates for social media positions are early adopters of technology, so if you camped outside your local Apple store to be first in line for the newest iPhone, try to bring that up during your job interview.

The following is just a sampling of the many new positions in the industry now open to job seekers who are passionate about social media. The descriptions of these positions are intended to be general, since the specific responsibilities for each job will most likely differ from one company to another.

COMMUNITY MANAGER

Community managers help businesses by building a strong online community of fans, friends, and followers. The position usually involves managing a company's communications and writing content. Community managers create blog posts, newsletters, articles, and other types of material for social media channels, so good writing skills are essential. Many handle customer support, such as managing online feedback forums. They often attend industry events and organize community meet-ups, and they establish relationships with industry journalists. In addition to being Internet savvy, good candidates for this position have outgoing personalities and are willing to work around the clock.

Professionals hired by businesses to help establish and maintain their online communities need to be outgoing individuals who enjoy socializing offline as well.

CONTENT CURATOR

Some people estimate that we will reach a point in the future when the quantity of information on the Web will double every seventy-two hours. A content curator's job is to sift through that growing mountain of content. He or she selects and repositions those elements best suited to an employer's social media platforms, such as articles, images, and viral videos. A content curator needs to be able to navigate the Web and distinguish the trash from the treasure.

ONLINE REPUTATION MANAGER

Negative content posted online, or "digital dirt," can have a damaging impact on the reputation of a person or business. This problem has led to the emergence of firms and consultants that help people and businesses erase unflattering content from the Web. Online reputation managers help people curate their online presence. They work to fill social platforms with positive reviews and posts in order to push negative results as far down as possible on the page of Google search results. In addition to possessing good PR skills, online reputation managers need to be well versed in search engine optimization (SEO).

Social Media Analyst

Social media analysts are responsible for creating and maintaining a business's presence on various social media platforms. They use SEO to increase the overall visibility of a company or brand on the Web, and they keep a close eye on trends in social media. They may also use tools such as Google Analytics to determine how effective a business's social media strategy is or determine if a particular social media campaign has achieved its goals. Social media analysts often bring a background in public relations, marketing, or social media management to this job.

Social Media Consultant

Social media consultants are outside consultants hired by businesses to get their social media efforts off the ground. A consultant might be responsible for developing an entire social media action strategy involving branding, logo, and Web site design. He or she might be brought in to teach groups of employees how to manage their Twitter accounts. Marketing experience comes in handy in this position, as well as knowing how to manage the development of online content on a company's various social media platforms. Social media consultants, like others in the industry, enjoy connecting with others both on- and offline.

SOCIAL MEDIA CUSTOMER SERVICE REPRESENTATIVE

If you are a naturally diplomatic person who genuinely enjoys helping people solve problems, then working as a social media customer service representative, or rep, might be a great online career for you. This job description includes answering questions, taking orders, and helping resolve customer complaints via online chat. The customer service rep wants to make sure that a customer's experiences with a particular company or brand are ultimately positive ones. As in other customer service positions, this is a job where it pays to be personable, professional, and able to keep one's cool even when a customer is upset. Fast typing skills are definitely an asset.

SOCIAL MEDIA TRAINING FOR EMPLOYEES

Just as many companies now require ethics and diversity training for new employees, human resources departments have awakened to the importance of providing social media training for all new hires. Firms expect their employees to be literate in social media, not just to prevent fiascos where workers badmouth the company in public online forums, but because they believe knowing how to navigate social

The orientation process for many new employees now includes training sessions in the uses and ethics of various types of social media.

networks will increase their employees' productivity and job performance.

SOCIAL MEDIA INTERNSHIPS

Teenagers probably have more experience with Facebook and Twitter than many of the people who are looking to hire them. A social media internship can further enhance your résumé, earn you college credit, and help position you for a career in social media. Many companies hire summer interns, but competition for these positions can be fierce. The kind of positive digital footprint and networking strategies that can help employers and recruiters locate you online will also make a person an attractive candidate for an internship.

The top qualities that employers look for in an intern include excellent writing and social skills, as well as creativity, enthusiasm, and a willingness to work hard. It should go without saying that a person must have an active online presence (a blog, a Twitter following, a Pinterest page) and know his or her way around various social networking platforms.

Some companies pay their interns, but many do not. As is the case with any internship, some are better than others. Ideally, interns should develop new skills, make useful business contacts, and acquire valuable experience to include on a résumé. According to a recent survey of these positions, an intern may even be asked to design and execute the entire social media strategy for a company! You don't want to spend your summer doing endless Google searches for clients, so read the job description carefully and ask good questions about what your responsibilities will be before committing yourself.

WORKING FROM HOME

David Karp, founder and CEO of the blogging site Tumblr, landed his first major job when he was just seventeen years old. Karp was hired as the chief technology officer for the Web site UrbanBaby because his boss never interviewed Karp in person and had no clue he was so young. Soon after he was hired, Karp moved to Japan and continued doing his job from there without his employer ever finding out.

Thanks to evolving digital technologies, many of the new jobs in social media allow employees to work either

INTERNET EMPLOYMENT SCAMS

If the idea of working from home seems too good to be true, sometimes it is. Be warned that some work-from-home (WFH) or work-at-home (WAH) jobs are actually scams designed to target students, homemakers, seniors, and disabled people, among others. Unfortunately, many people have been taken in by such bogus offers and have ended up losing large sums of money. The prevalence of these scams has made it more difficult for legitimate work-from-home businesses to operate. Learning how to recognize an Internet employment scam can prevent you from falling for one.

You can spot these scams because they usually appear in your spam filter from out of nowhere. Many feature loud graphics and testimonials from people who claim they made "THOUSANDS OF DOLLARS!!!!!!" working from home. Scammers often stress that they are making a limited-time offer, and you will lose the opportunity if you don't act immediately. They promise huge amounts of money for doing very simple tasks.

Common scams jobs involve envelope stuffing, package forwarding, rebate processing, medical billing, and discount or coupon programs.

partly or entirely from home—or from practically any-where. All of the jobs profiled here can be accomplished remotely. Bloggers, online forum moderators, Facebook and Twitter marketing assistants, social media research-ers, and virtual assistants can—and often do—work from home, or the local Starbucks. While misleading a potential employer, as David Karp did, is never a good idea, having a job where you interact entirely online with your boss or clients has numerous advantages for you, as well as for the

Before he launched the blogging platform Tumblr, which sold to Yahoo! for $1.1 billion, CEO David Karp ran a Web site from his mother's Manhattan apartment.

planet. When you only have to commute from your bed to your desk, you don't waste hours each week sitting in freeway traffic or risking your life in the fast lane. Working from home dramatically reduces your carbon footprint as well as your employer's. You can also save thousands of dollars a year on transportation costs, and you don't need to spend money on a work wardrobe.

Jobs where you work from home online often allow more flexibility than in-house staff positions. Sometimes you can set your own hours, which is a great advantage if you have other responsibilities such as attending classes or taking care of a family, or if you're a night owl who gets more done later in the day. For extremely shy or introverted people, communicating via e-mail and social networks may be a chance to express their ideas more clearly and with greater force than while under the pressure of person-to-person interaction. Working online opens up a world of employment possibilities for individuals with speech or hearing impairments or other disabilities.

Traditionally, job seekers have had to move to where the jobs were, leaving rural areas to congregate in cities, traveling far from their friends and families, and uprooting spouses and children in the process. Partners with different professional backgrounds might find it difficult to find equally satisfying work in the same area. Being able to work online means that you can do your job from almost anywhere that Internet service is available. You don't necessarily need more than basic computer skills to work remotely, either. User-friendly programs have made it easy for almost anyone to quickly gain mastery of social networks, conduct Internet searches, start a blog, build a Web site, send and receive electronic files and images, and perform many other tasks.

In recent years, many industries have suffered financial woes. Companies have had to downsize and outsource work, and employees have felt less secure in their jobs than ever before. Amid this atmosphere of economic uncertainty, the robust growth of the social media industry has been an encouraging sign, especially for young people who have the social networking skills that forward-thinking employers need.

CHAPTER 4

USING ONLINE NETWORKS TO LAND OFF-LINE JOBS

Since the personal computer revolutionized how people function, many formerly hands-on professions have become increasingly dependent on software programs. Workers have had to learn computer skills to adapt to the changing demands of their jobs. For instance, rather than spending days out in the field gathering samples, many environmental scientists now work indoors at a desk with aerial photos, computer-generated maps, and models. Mechanical engineers, animators, fashion designers, architects, and others who formerly accomplished most of their tasks by hand now rely on computer programs.

Not everyone aspires to spend his or her working life in front of a computer, however. Despite the surging popularity of social networks, a recent "Common Sense Media Research Study" showed that most teens prefer to socialize face-to-face, and they believe that social media can interfere with that. You may enjoy connecting with your friends online but dream of a career that doesn't chain you to a desk, a job where you hike on mountain trails, build

FROM BLOGS TO BOOKS

One way that social media can lead to a more traditional offline job is the phenomenon of the blog-turned-book deal. Originally dismissed as online journals or rants, blogs have become important features of the cyberverse. Influential bloggers attract large audiences that may include book publishers, who recognize the opportunity to turn a popular blog into something more substantial…and profitable.

Julie Powell turned her passion into a blog that became a book, and eventually, a movie. A big fan of the famous chef Julia Child, Powell created a blog that chronicled her attempts to cook every one of Child's recipes. The blog soon developed a large following and earned Powell a book deal with a major publisher. Then her book was made into the 2009 movie *Julie & Julia* starring Amy Adams and Meryl Streep. Advice columns, collections of tweets, and Web sites featuring funny pictures of cats have all been made into books as well.

fine furniture, or play stand-up bass in a jazz band. Take heart—there are still plenty of hands-on jobs to be had. Careers in construction, physical education, and the culinary arts, to name just a few, are all great routes for individuals who don't want to spend their time slaving over a hot computer keyboard.

The social networking phenomenon has been around long enough now that people working in all types of fields have come to recognize how useful these networks can be. Educators turn to social networks to share their war stories from the front lines of the classroom and pick each other's brains about how to reach at-risk students. An American band on tour in Germany can go online to find an alto saxophonist to play a last-minute club booking in Frankfurt. Popular and well-established social networks like Facebook, LinkedIn, Twitter, and Google+ are all excellent sources for finding offline jobs. Establishing profiles on these sites should definitely be part of an overall job search strategy. However, many alternative social networks exist that are targeted toward people in more specialized careers or fields. Bearing in mind that the cyber landscape can change overnight, what follows are some good sources for specialized social networks in various industries.

CONSTRUCTION

According to Construction Marketing Advisors, LinkedIn and Twitter are the most effective social networking platforms for the construction industry, so you'll want to start there. Another useful site to investigate is Built.com, a social network for job seekers, employers, and professionals working in architecture,

Social networks geared toward specific career paths enable job seekers to find work in the construction business and other hands-on professions.

engineering, construction, building management, and related jobs, often referred to as A/E/C professions.

CULINARY ARTS

Founded in 2006, BakeSpace has been called "Facebook for foodies." Members can connect with a global community of other food enthusiasts, home cooks, and people working (or planning to work) in the culinary arts to share recipes, ideas, and expertise. One great feature of BakeSpace is its Mentor Program, where volunteers possessing specific culinary skills offer to share them with other members. Other social networks that cater to foodies include BigOven, Foodpals.com, and Nibbledish.

FINE ARTS

Image-heavy online networks such as Flickr, Tumblr, and Pinterest (which has been described as a visual Twitter) have all attracted thriving artistic communities and are excellent resources for creative individuals. DeviantArt claims to be "the world's largest online community of artists and art lovers," with more than twenty-five million registered artists and art appreciators; the site features plenty of tutorials, indicating that its community is committed to sharing knowledge. Two additional popular social networks for artists are ArtSlant and Behance.

GREEN JOBS

Care2.com, a well-established networking site with over twenty-one million members, enables users to search for green jobs, support a variety of social causes, sign online petitions, and join or create an interest group. Wiser.org, "the social network of sustainability," connects users with other members committed to creating a more just and sustainable world, and it features a searchable job list.

MEDICINE

Some of the best-known social networks for those in the medical profession, such as Doximity and Sermo, are open

Health care is a career field that continues to see growth. Online job boards show that positions in the medical and dental professions pay well and are in high demand.

only to physicians and other health care professionals, but MedicalMingle is for anyone interested in a career in health care or the medical field. The site offers job postings, blogging, and career resources.

MUSIC AND THE PERFORMING ARTS

Perhaps because making music is often a deeply collaborative enterprise, any Internet search will turn up many social sites specifically for musicians and people in the music industry. For a decade, Myspace provided musicians and other creative people with an excellent online platform for their endeavors. Myspace allowed users to incorporate multimedia elements into their profiles, letting a musician create a page nearly as engaging as a live performance. The site relaunched in 2013 as the New Myspace, to a chilly reception. It remains to be seen whether or not the revamped Myspace will retain its membership.

New to the scene is Fandalism.com. Members of this network can share their work through images and embedded videos, connect with other musicians all over the world, give "props" to their performances, and send each other messages.

Actors and others employed in the performing arts, or those interested in a career in this field, can connect with others, critique each other's performance videos, and review job postings and casting calls at sites such as ActingSoup .com, ActorsConnect.com, HowsMyActing.com, and the Contemporary Performance Network.

Once considered the top social media site for musicians, Myspace (www.myspace.com) is now one of many online networks dedicated to serving people in the music and entertainment business.

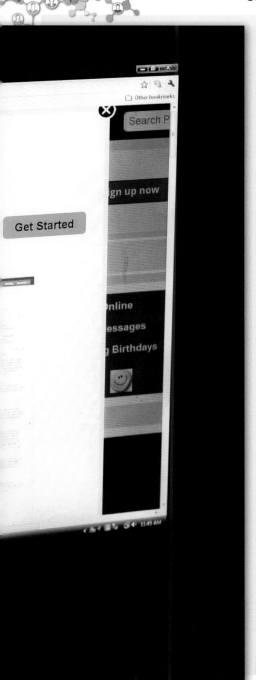

NONPROFITS

People committed to making the world a better place often begin their job search in the nonprofit sector, where social media has transformed the nature of philanthropy and fundraising. People working in this field can link up on commercial social networks such as Facebook, as well as house social networks hosted by nonprofit organizations themselves. Compared to Facebook and Twitter, the popularity of LinkedIn among nonprofit professionals is relatively low, according to a recent nonprofit social network survey sponsored by Common Knowledge.

SELF-EMPLOYED WORKERS

Over the past three years, online hiring and freelancing increased more than 200 percent, according to Elance, an online employment marketplace. Companies that can't afford to hire employees full-time often hire freelancers, and firms that have had to downsize frequently hire former employees on a contract basis. Freelance workers, known legally as independent contractors, are represented in nearly all professions, from trucking and interior design to landscaping and information technology.

Professional networks such as LinkedIn have become key resources for those who work independently or from home. Increasing one's visibility on various social networks is an essential strategy for freelancers, who are always on the hunt for the next job. The networks you join will depend on the particular type of freelance work you do. Being your own boss comes at the price of paying for your own health care and retirement accounts. Freelancers usually don't get

Many freelance workers, sometimes called project-based personnel, post their work profiles and search for jobs through online self-employment marketplaces such as Elance.

paid for their vacation time and often work on weekends. Belonging to a network where members offer advice and support about how to meet such challenges can help independent workers succeed.

This represents just a small sampling of hands-on professions that use social networks to share employment information and job listings. Determined job seekers should not limit themselves to these few Web sites, but should search online and see what else they can find there. The time a job hunter invests in cultivating online relationships may be precisely what helps him or her to craft a rewarding future career...one that doesn't include a desk job and a computer screen.

CHAPTER 5

TOMORROW'S JOB SEARCH

Current innovations in job searching would have been unthinkable twenty-five years ago. Similarly, we can't begin to imagine what new developments will transform the playing field in the years to come. Still, employment experts believe that the following trends will have an important impact on the future of recruiting.

MOBILE RECRUITING

Mobile Internet use is projected to surpass desktop use in the next couple of years. More people than ever will access social networks on their phones and iPads while in a movie theater ticket line or in the waiting room at the dentist's office. Recruiters see mobile technologies as a great tool for human resources. They look forward to the day when job candidates will not only search for work on a mobile device but will also apply for a job with just one click.

Mobile technologies may eventually allow job applicants to see up-to-the-minute data on how they compare to other candidates applying for the same position. Messages announcing that certain positions are closed will automatically be forwarded to applicants' mobile devices. A

Some companies reward employees who refer successful job candidates from among their own social groups. Employees referred by friends often remain longer at a company than those who apply independently.

recorded video interview with a candidate could easily be shared with other staff members involved in the hiring decision. In the Unites States, where significantly more African Americans and Hispanics than Caucasians access the Internet on mobile devices, employers could potentially connect with a more diverse pool of talent. Recruiters believe that mobile devices will eventually streamline all stages of the recruiting process for employers and job seekers.

PEER-TO-PEER RECRUITING AND JOB BOUNTIES

Current employees have always been a great source of new talent for any organization. They can alert friends and family when positions open up and provide them with recommendations. The power of social media can help this type of peer-to-peer recruitment go viral, enabling employees to use their own social networks as a recruiting tool. Some online recruitment networks offer job bounties as an incentive: an individual who succeeds in referring an applicant who secures a job offer earns a cash bonus.

THE RÉSUMÉ, REINVENTED

Some human resource managers will say that the one-page paper résumé is obsolete and has been replaced by innovations such as visual résumés and "Twit-Fit" résumés—the résumé reimagined as a series of Twitter updates. Visual résumés illustrate a job seeker's credentials using infographics, word clouds, timelines, slide presentations, and other eye-catching techniques. One job seeker redesigned his résumé to resemble a subway map. Such creative résumés may be the most appropriate for applicants looking for work in creative industries, however, and the visual design should never interfere with the clear presentation of information.

Another twist on the traditional résumé is the video résumé, where a job seeker films and posts his or her résumé on YouTube or another video-sharing site. Plenty of sites provide online video profiles that job hunters can use. Video résumés demonstrate to a potential employer that an applicant knows how to use basic video technology. Furthermore, if an individual comes across well on camera, a video résumé may compensate for his or her lack of experience on paper. On the other hand, not everyone projects his or her personality well through this medium. If the idea of producing a video

Fallon Rechnitz, a student at Arizona State University, created a video résumé on WorkBlast (www.workblast.com) that highlights her education and job skills, as well as her technological savvy.

résumé appeals to you, do a test run to see how successfully you come across, and get honest feedback from your friends and family.

Public relations and social media consultant Graeme Anthony used his skills to create an interactive video résumé with links to sections labeled "About Me," "Skills," and "Timeline," which he posted on YouTube. His résumé attracted so many job offers that rather than accepting a staff position with one company, he decided to become an independent consultant.

Gamification and Contest Applications

Lovers of video games, rejoice! In acknowledgment of the popularity of video gaming, especially among digital natives, one of the most exciting innovations in social recruiting is "gamification"—taking the essence of video gaming and applying it to real-world problems. The growing gamification industry integrates gaming dynamics and mechanics into non-game applications, such as designing ways for people to solve business problems in game environments.

Gamification is being used in human resources to recruit, train, and engage workers, helping attract more young job applicants to various industries. Anyone who plays video games knows how addicting they can be. Gamification applications tap into the sense of competitiveness that you feel when you're playing a video game. They motivate you with rewards that encourage you to progress through various gaming levels, often

BEST PRACTICES FOR JOB SEEKERS

- Watch your language. Don't use profanity or communicate sloppily or in text speak, and proofread everything you post online. Some people have the mistaken idea that e-mails and online comments are informal communications and that spelling errors don't really matter. They're wrong. Don't give a potential employer or job contact any reason to eliminate you from the running. Take every opportunity to demonstrate your attention to detail.

- Be consistent. If you're on Twitter, tweet every day. If your presence on social media comes in sporadic little bursts, with long silences in between, this will suggest that you're not fully engaged.

- Communicate your passions. Enthusiasm is infectious, and an interested person is always more interesting to others. A potential employer or someone who might recommend you for a job wants to know that you have the capacity to care about your work.

- Be honest. Never lie about your credentials and accomplishments.

- Think "we," not "me." Finally, remember that social networking is all about building mutually beneficial relationships. When you're looking to connect with people you hope can help advance your career, don't just think in terms of what they can do for you, but of what you have to offer them and the larger community.

working with a team toward a shared goal. As part of its effort to recruit new employees, Marriott International developed a hotel-themed online game in which the player takes the role of a virtual kitchen manager and has to balance all of the many responsibilities of that position. *My Marriott Hotel* on Facebook introduces the player to the hotel industry and shows how exciting the hospitality industry can be.

Companies also use contests and challenges to attract the best job candidates. Contests allow applicants to set themselves apart with their ideas, creativity, and aptitude, while learning directly about a company's priorities, goals, and mission. As part of its recruitment strategy, MasterCard ran a "Cashless Society" campaign. Applicants were challenged to use a social media site to demonstrate what a cashless society meant to them. An organization can also host a contest as a means of raising its profile in the community.

Creating a favorable impression through online networking can complement, but never replace, the impression a successful job seeker makes in person.

Importance of Offline Networking

It's important to remember, despite having all of these incredible digital networking tools at your fingertips, that they should not replace but should complement traditional offline networking. It takes time to build relationships with people, and time spent conversing face-to-face or over the telephone will almost always be well spent and ultimately more effective for the job seeker than exclusively online communications.

In recognition of the need for actual (as opposed to virtual) interaction, many social networks host events or "meetups" to enable fellow users to get to know one another in person. Twitter organizers can schedule "tweetups." Industry conferences, such as Social Media Week, provide opportunities for people to bring their online connections offline and network face-to-face.

Obviously you won't be able to actually meet every person that you communicate with online, and younger users should exercise extreme caution in this regard. But it's important to nurture some key relationships and take them beyond the virtual world into the real one. Arranging to meet someone whom you have built a good connection with online can go a long way toward helping you stand out from the crowd of other eager job seekers. Enabling someone to put a face to your name ("Oh, you're the person who posted those great tweets") will definitely help people remember you. It will also show that you consider them important enough to meet in

person. Making this kind of good impression can be invaluable to your career, and you never know where it will lead.

When Apple Inc.'s founder and visionary CEO, the late Steve Jobs, was thirteen, he looked up Bill Hewlett's number in the phonebook, called him, and asked the founder of Hewlett-Packard (HP) if he could help him get some parts for an electronic device that he wanted to build. In the course of their conversation, Hewlett was so impressed by the young man that he offered him a summer job in the instruments division of HP. That's an example of the power of offline social networking—and a useful reminder that social networks have been around a lot longer than the Internet. Thanks to Jobs, and to other world-changing innovators like him, teens can now take advantage of numerous digital tools to help them find employment. But there is no still no virtual equivalent for a firm handshake.

GLOSSARY

curate To select and organize items in a collection or exhibition; to thoughtfully choose and arrange online content.

digital dirt Unflattering information about a person that can be found on the Internet.

digital footprint The trail an individual leaves in cyberspace or on any form of digital communication.

gamification The integration of game mechanics or dynamics into non-game applications to make them more fun and engaging.

hashtag Any phrase that follows the pound symbol (#) in a tweet, used to categorize tweets by topic.

job board A physical or virtual area that lists available jobs; a Web site that facilitates job hunting.

keyword A word typed in to begin an online search.

microblogging A form of blogging that allows users to write and publish brief text updates, usually no more than about two hundred characters long.

post A message entered into a network, such as a blog, discussion group, social networking site, or online forum; also used as a verb, as in "to post."

profile A user's online page that contains her or his personal information.

search engine optimization (SEO) A technique that helps search engines find and rank Web sites by searching for keywords. SEO experts know how to make adjustments to the HTML code of a Web site so that an Internet search will find a site quickly.

Skype A software application that allows users to make voice and video calls over the Internet.

social recruiting When companies and recruiters use Facebook, LinkedIn, Twitter, and other social networks to source and recruit job candidates.

spam Unsolicited electronic messages, usually advertising a product or service.

Common Sense Media
650 Townsend Street, Suite 375
San Francisco, CA 94103
(415) 863-0600
Web site: http://www
.commonsensemedia.org
Common Sense Media is a nonprofit organization that provides
tools and information to help
parents make informed choices
about the media kids use.

CoolWorks
P.O. Box 272
513 Highway 89
Gardiner, MN 59030
(406) 848-1195
Web site: http://www
.coolworks.com
CoolWorks is a Web site that
lists summer and seasonal jobs,
as well as year-round positions in
national parks, ranches, camps,
ski resorts, and on cruise ships.

Icouldbe.org
25 East 21st Street, 6th Floor
New York, NY 10010
(917) 608-7093
Web site: http://www
.icouldbe.org
This innovative program matches
up at-risk middle and high school

students with an online community of professional mentors from
a variety of career fields.

Media Awareness Network
1500 Merivale Road, 3rd floor
Ottawa, ON K2E 6Z5
Canada
(613) 224-7721
Web site: http://www
.media-awareness.ca
The Media Awareness Network
is a nonprofit committed to
teaching adults how media can
affect their children's lifestyles
and choices.

National Career Development
Association (NCDA)
305 N. Beech Circle
Broken Arrow, OK 74012
(866) 367-6232
Web site: http://www.ncda.org
The NCDA is the first and
longest-running career development association in the world.

Social Safety.org
280 Union Square Drive
New Hope, PA 18938
Web site: http://www
.socialsafety.org
Funded by Microsoft and

designed by MyYearbook's teen founders, Dave and Catherine Cook, this program helps inform teens about the potential dangers of social networking.

Youth Canada
140 Promenade du Portage, Phase IV, 4D392
Mail Drop 403
Gatineau, QC K1A 0J9
Canada
(800) 965-5555
Web site: http://www.youth.gc.ca
Sponsored by the Canadian government, this site features a youth blog and many resources for teen job seekers.

WEB SITES

Due to the changing nature of Internet links, Rosen Publishing has developed an online list of Web sites related to the subject of this book. This site is updated regularly. Please use this link to access the list:

http://www.rosenlinks.com/TGPSN/Emply

Awl, Dave. *Facebook Me! A Guide to Socializing, Sharing, and Promoting on Facebook.* 2nd ed. Berkeley, CA: Peachpit Press, 2011.

Cook, Colleen Ryckert. *Frequently Asked Questions About Social Networking* (Teen Life). New York, NY: Rosen Publishing, 2011.

Espejo, Roman. *Social Networking* (Teen Rights and Freedoms). Farmington Hills, MI: Gale Group, 2011.

Hillstrom, Laurie Collier. *Online Social Networks.* Farmington Hills, MI: Lucent Books 2010.

Hussey, Tris. *Create Your Own Blog: Six Easy Projects to Start Blogging Like a Pro.* Indianapolis, IN: Sams Publishing, 2010.

Jacubiak, David. J. *A Smart Kid's Guide to Social Networking Online.* New York, NY: PowerKids Press, 2010.

Labovich, Laura M., and Miriam Saltpeter. *100 Conversations for Career Success: Learn to Network, Cold Call, and Tweet Your Way to Your Dream Job.* New York, NY: LearningExpress, 2012.

Lusted, Marcia Aidon. *Social Networking: MySpace, Facebook, and Twitter.* Edina: MN: ABDO Publishing, 2011.

McFedries, Paul. *Twitter Tips, Tricks, and Tweets.* 2nd ed. Hoboken, NJ: Wiley, 2010.

Obee, Jennifer. *Social Networking: The Ultimate Teen Guide.* Lanham, MD: Scarecrow Press, 2012.

O'Reilly, Tim, and Sarah Milstein. *The Twitter Book.* 2nd ed. Sebastopol, CA: O'Reilly Media, 2012.

Raatma, Lucia. *Social Networks* (21st Century Skills). Ann Arbor, MI: Cherry Lake Publishing, 2010.

Ryan, Peter K. *Social Networking.* New York, NY: Rosen Publishing, 2011.

Tieger, Paul D., et al. *Do What You Are: Discover the Perfect Career for You Through the Secrets of Personality Type.* New York, NY: Little, Brown & Company, 2007.

BIBLIOGRAPHY

Ayelet, Noff. "The Starbucks Formula for Social Media Success." Next Web, January 11, 2010. Retrieved February 5, 2013 (http://www.thenextweb.com).

Casserly, Meghan. "Social Media and the Job Hunt: Squeaky-Clean Profiles Need Not Apply." *Forbes*, June 14, 2012. Retrieved January 23, 2013 (http://www.forbes.com).

Common Knowledge. *4th Annual Nonprofit Social Network Benchmark Report 2012*. Retrieved February 5, 2013 (http://www.nonprofitsocialnetwork-survey.com).

Common Sense Media Research Study. "Social Media, Social Life: How Teens View Their Digital Lives." July 26, 2012. Retrieved January 18, 2012 (http://www.commonsensemedia.org).

Crompton, Diane, and Ellen Sautter, *Find a Job Through Social Networking*. Indianapolis, IN: JIST Works, 2011.

Gross, Doug. "Are Social Media Making the Résumé Obsolete?" CNN, July 11, 2012. Retrieved January 28, 2013 (http://www.cnn.com).

Meister, Jeanne. "The Death of the Résumé." *Forbes*, July 23, 2012. Retrieved February 6, 2013 (http://www.forbes.com).

Meister, Jeanne. "Gamification: Three Ways to Use Gaming for Recruiting, Training, and Health & Wellness." *Forbes*, May 21, 2012. Retrieved February 6, 2013 (http://www.forbes.com).

Popkin, Helen A. S. "Facebook Hits 1 Billion Users." Digital Life, October 4, 2012. Retrieved February 2, 2013 (http://digitallife.today.com).

Salpeter, Miriam. *Social Networking for Career Success*. New York, NY: Learning Express, 2011.

Schepp, Brad, and Debra Schepp. *How to Find a Job on LinkedIn, Facebook, Twitter, MySpace, and Other Social*

Networks. New York, NY: McGraw-Hill, 2010.

Schwabel, Dan. "How Job Seekers Are Using Social Networks." Open Forum, December 12, 2012. Retrieved January 16, 2012 (http://www.openforum.com/articles/how-job-seekers-are-using-social-networks-to-find-work).

Sharma, Praful. "How Disney and 5 Other Top Employers Use Twitter to Recruit." Undercover Recruiter. Retrieved January 30, 2012 (http://www.theundercoverrecruiter.com/how-disney-and-5-other-top-employers-use-twitter-to-recruit).

Smith, Catharine, and Craig Kanally. "Fired Over Facebook: 13 Posts That Got People CANNED." *Huffington Post*, July 26, 2010. Retrieved January 20, 2013 (http://www.huffingtonpost.com).

Spark, David. "16 Wishes for Future Mobile Recruiting." Dice, November 14, 2012. Retrieved February 7, 2013 (http://resources.dice.com/2012/11/14/16-wishes-for-future-mobile-recruiting).

Sullivan, Dr. John. "Next Year's Recruiting Headlines, Trends, and Next Practices." Ere.net, November 5, 2012. Retrieved January 29, 2012 (http://www.ere.net).

Valkenburg, Jacco. "93% of Recruiters Use Social Media in 2012, Up from 87% in 2011." Global Recruiting Roundtable, July 16, 2012. Retrieved January 23, 2012 (http://www.globalrecruitinground table.com).

Waldman, Joshua. *Job Searching with Social Media for Dummies*. Hoboken, NJ: For Dummies, 2011.

Whitcomb, Susan Britton, et al. *The Twitter Job Search Guide: Find a Job and Advance Your Career in Just 15 Minutes a Day*. Indianapolis, IN: JIST Works, 2010.

INDEX

ABOUT THE AUTHOR

Monique Vescia is a writer with many nonfiction books to her credit. Her previous book was *David Karp and Tumblr*, about the founder of the social networking site.

PHOTO CREDITS

Cover (left), p. 4 © iStockphoto.com/Jaroslaw Wojcik; cover (right) © iStockphoto.com/Momcilog; cover, p. 1 (screen) © iStockphoto.com/andrearoad; cover, pp. 1, 8, 24, 36, 49, 61 (background icons) © iStockphoto.com/Matt Chalwell; p. 4 (background) © iStockphoto.com/Danil Melekhin; p. 5 © iStockphoto.com/contrastaddict; p. 6 Comstock/Thinkstock; p. 9 © Canadian Press/AP Images; pp. 11, 28 Bloomberg/Getty Images; p. 13 Dominic Lipinski/Press Association/AP Images; p. 15 Stephen Lam/Getty Images; p. 22 Jochen Tack/ imagebroker.net/SuperStock; p. 25 Yuri Arcurs/Shutterstock .com; pp. 30–31 Camera Press/James Veysey/Redux; p. 34 Karen Bleier/AFP/Getty Images; pp. 38–39, 62–63 iStockphoto/ Thinkstock; pp. 42–43 Zoran Mircetic/E+/Getty Images; p. 46 Nadine Rupp/Getty Images; p. 52 Blend Images/Shutterstock; p. 54 Gergely Zsolnai/Shutterstock.com; pp. 56–57, 65 © AP Images; pp. 58–59 Araya Diaz/Getty Images; p. 68–69 Thoels Graugaard/the Agency Collection/Getty Images; additional social networking icons © iStockphoto.com/P2007; network graphic © iStockphoto.com/imagotres.

Designer: Nelson Sá; Editor: Nicholas Croce; Photo Researcher: Marty Levick